Companions on the Journey

Companions on the Journey

Foundational Spiritual Practices

Tracey D. Leslie

RESOURCE *Publications* · Eugene, Oregon

COMPANIONS ON THE JOURNEY
Foundational Spiritual Practices

Resource Publications
An Imprint of Wipf and Stock Publishers
199 W. 8th Ave., Suite 3
Eugene, OR 97401

www.wipfandstock.com

PAPERBACK ISBN: 978-1-5326-9832-3
HARDCOVER ISBN: 978-1-5326-9833-0
EBOOK ISBN: 978-1-5326-9834-7

Manufactured in the U.S.A.   DECEMBER 5, 2019

To my husband, Britt: I am thankful to God that he is my companion on my life's journey.

Contents

Acknowledgements

SPIRITUAL PRACTICES AND GROUP spiritual formation have long been a passion for me. I am thankful to those who have provided me with opportunities in recent years to expand my knowledge and experience in this area. Thanks to Rev. Dan Gildner, DMin, former Professor of Spiritual Formation at United Theological Seminary in Dayton, Ohio. The opportunity to serve as a spiritual formation facilitator with seminary students was crucial to my own growth. Dan's knowledge, mentorship, and willingness to dialogue with me regarding issues surrounding group spiritual formation were deeply appreciated.

This experience inspired my desire for continued growth and learning and led to my application to the Spiritual Direction Internship through Benedict Inn in Beech Grove, Indiana. I am especially thankful to the program's director, Sister Antoinette Purcell, OSB, and my peer group directors, Sister Wanda Wetli, CSJ and Sister Barbara Leonhard, OFS.

Much gratitude, as well, to my spiritual director, Brother Daniel Chad Hoffman, CG. His direction and encouragement kept me moving forward with this project.

This group study in foundational spiritual practices was many years in the making and iterations were shared with small groups in the United Methodist congregations I served over those years. Many thanks to the congregations at Castleton United Methodist Church in Indianapolis, Indiana and Trinity United Methodist Church in Lafayette, Indiana. Your willingness to engage these spiritual practices with authenticity and openness and to provide honest feedback was crucial in developing this resource.

I am thankful for Rev. Andrew Kinsey, DMin, whose experience in publishing was a true blessing as I navigated this inaugural journey as an author. I am deeply appreciative for my copyeditor and friend, Allegra W. Smith, for her expert work in preparing this publication.

Most of all, words could not express my appreciation for my husband and partner, Rev. Britt Leslie, PhD. I rely deeply on his biblical scholarship and research, as well as on his encouragement and support. I am doubly blessed.

Introduction

Welcome to Companions on the Journey

To the group participants:

I BELIEVE THAT CHRISTIANITY is, first and foremost, about relationship: our relationship with God through Jesus Christ. How then do we develop and nurture our relationship with Jesus? Certainly the grace of God in Christ is nothing we can earn or manipulate. It is a gift. But there are things we can do to open ourselves to God's grace; to make our lives like fertile soil. These are, traditionally, known as spiritual practices, and they are often best practiced in the context of Christian community.

In this study, we'll engage with some foundational spiritual practices that can help us grow in our relationships with God and one another. Whether you are just beginning a relationship with Jesus or seeking to deepen a more mature relationship, I pray you will find these practices valuable as have Christians across the centuries and around the world.

Because Christianity is, primarily, a vibrant relationship and not a stagnant set of beliefs, *session one* begins by employing the metaphor of a journey. As you read about the Old Testament patriarch, Abraham, you'll be encouraged to reflect on how God has been working and moving within you through the various stages of your life's journey thus far. You'll also be privileged to hear about the life experiences of your companions on this journey.

In *session two*, we will focus on the spiritual practice of reading, studying, and meditating on scripture. Through scripture, we come to know God, to know ourselves, and to understand the nature of the relationship God desires to have with us, as well as God's desires for our relationships with one another. By focusing on scripture as covenant, we understand its critical role in shaping and sustaining our relationship with God and one another.

In *session three*, we will explore prayer as fellowship with God: an ongoing and increasing awareness of God's presence. We'll make use of the Lord's Prayer as a model or pattern for our prayer lives. We'll consider types of prayer and experiment with different ways of praying that have been used by Christian saints across the centuries.

In *session four*, we will consider the spiritual practice of generosity. By examining some of Jesus' teaching as well as the teaching of Methodist founder, John Wesley, and contemporary theologians and church leaders, we'll consider how generosity reflects and impacts our relationship with Christ and one another.

The very word "evangelism" can leave us with impressions of intrusive missionaries ringing our doorbells at dinnertime or pushy people passing out tracts on street corners. In *session five*, we will be encouraged to write (or sketch) and share our spiritual autobiography: to share the good news of Christ by sharing the story of the difference Jesus has made in *our* lives. We will be challenged to reflect more deliberately upon our Christian journey and the gracious work of Christ within our lives so that we might share our story with others. The weekly reading will provide resources to assist with composing your spiritual autobiography through written word or pictures.

In the *final session*, we will consider God's call upon our lives and the gifts, skills, and talents that God has given us in order that we might fulfill our call. We'll discuss ways to discover, discern, and affirm spiritual gifts within ourselves and our companions on this journey.

Unless otherwise indicated, all Scripture quotations are from the New Revised Standard Version Bible (NRSV).

To the group facilitator:

I have chosen the title "facilitator" deliberately. It is not assumed that you will have more information or knowledge than other group participants. You will not be expected to teach or instruct; rather your role will be one of spiritual guide. Throughout this study, you'll be encouraged to *cultivate Christian covenant community*.

To *cultivate* means to create environmental conditions conducive to growth. There is a subtle distinction between learning and growth. Learning may add to our bank of knowledge without necessarily changing us. Growth means actual change. However, we cannot force or control growth. In your role as facilitator, you can cultivate an environment (a group dynamic) conducive to growth by modeling openness, honesty, and respect.

This is a *Christian* study. Even when examining Hebrew (Old Testament) scripture, we do so from a Christian perspective. This study does not pass judgment on other faith traditions but is clearly focused on developing a relationship with God through Jesus as we deepen our understanding of who Jesus is, what Jesus taught, what Jesus did, and how Jesus lived.

During the first meeting, you will lead your group in entering into *covenant* with one another (see Appendix C). Covenants are commitments made in the context of relationship. The covenant included with this study is the primary tool for cultivating a group environment that is open, honest, and respectful. In your role as facilitator, keeping your group participants mindful of this sacred covenant will be essential for participants' growth.

As covenant is maintained and trust grows, a sense of Christian *community* develops. In a context of authentic community, people move beyond sharing ideas and opinions; they begin to share themselves and their experiences with one another.

Since each group is unique, you will want to read one session ahead before each meeting to prepare yourself as the facilitator. Each week's session includes *a 4–5 page participant reading to be completed in advance of the group meeting.* Participants should receive the book in advance and should complete the first week's participant reading in advance of the first group meeting. Although weekly readings are brief, remind participants that each reading includes reflection questions that they should answer. Therefore, they should complete the reading well in advance of the group meeting. "Cramming" the weekly reading will hamper their ability to participate in the group discussion and undermine the integrity of the group's covenant.

Because group discussion is fundamental to this study's goal—to cultivate Christian covenant community—the recommended group size is 8–10 participants. Furthermore, regular attendance is critical. Certainly, emergencies (such as illness) happen. But sporadic, irregular attendance by even one group participant can undermine the development of trust within the group. Although learning is often easily done "remotely" (through online studies and courses, for example), developing authentic community is not something we can "phone in." It requires regular, personal engagement with one another. Furthermore, as the series progresses, group discussions call for greater spiritual openness and deeper trust among participants.

A note about the weekly prayer:

Each week when you gather, you will open with a set format that includes prayer. Participants will be invited to name a prayer concern *as you pray together*. This design is purposeful for three reasons. First, when we list prayer concerns before prayer begins, it easily becomes a lengthy process. It may involve significant cross talking and people may use it as a time to "catch up" on one another's lives. A brief prayer time can stretch across several minutes before the prayer has even begun! Prayer is important. Christian fellowship is important. However, individuals have joined this group for an express purpose. Each week's session should be approximately 75–90 minutes in duration. When people are intensely present, engaged, and attentive, 75 minutes can be a long time! As facilitator, you honor participants and the covenant entered into by using time appropriately. Second, many Christians feel apprehensive about praying in a group. By inviting them to simply share a name and/or concern, you are helping them to grow in their prayer maturity. They need not look to the facilitator to voice their concern on their behalf. Finally, we must always remember that we bring our concerns to God with trust, believing that God knows all things. We need not give God the "back story," describe the current conditions, or elaborate on our anticipated results. God knows, understands, and will respond because of God's gracious, faithful nature.

Although, as facilitator, you are not required or expected to be an expert, if you would like some additional tools for biblical and theological preparation and reflection, a list of resources is provided at the conclusion of the leader's guide, session two.

Let the journey begin . . .

Participant Guide

Weekly Reading

Session 1

Faith: More a Journey than a Destination

EARLY IN OUR MARRIAGE, my husband and I took a trip out west. I'm a Pennsylvania native and I had never been any farther west than Indianapolis. I purchased tickets on the Amtrak Southwest Chief. It originated in Chicago and ended in California (though we only had enough money to make it to Albuquerque, New Mexico). I was enthralled with Chicago, especially the traffic. We had neither the time nor the money to go to the top of the Sears Tower—but it was pretty impressive, even from street level. We boarded the train in the evening and journeyed through the night. Early the next morning, when the sun came up, I went up to the observation car. I had never seen prairie before (except on TV's *Little House on the Prairie*!). It was breathtaking. So flat you could see for miles; vast, open prairie filled with prairie grass and wild flowers. Every so often, we would roll past a cattle yard; but mostly, it was prairie grass and wild flowers. I put my feet up, put on my headphones, and popped Copland's *Rodeo* into my Walkman. It was an amazing experience.

Life is a journey: a journey of joy and sorrow, calm and storms, successes and losses, solitude and companionship, doing and being. Likewise, our spiritual life is also a journey. Our relationship with God is dynamic: continually changing as our experiences and emotions provoke us to engage with God in different ways.

In scripture, God's people are continually on the move. In the Book of Exodus, God speaks to Moses from a burning bush and calls him to lead the Israelite people out of their enslavement in Egypt. They are to journey through the wilderness toward a new land: a good and fertile land called Canaan. As the people journey through the wilderness, God gives the Israelites commandments (directions) to live by; these are instructions on how to worship him and guidelines for how to be in relationship with one another and those outside their community. Sometimes the people grumble and sometimes they give thanks; sometimes they listen and sometimes they disobey; sometimes they trust and sometimes they doubt.

When we read the gospel of Luke, we are invited to journey with Jesus and his disciples as they travel toward Jerusalem, the place where Jesus will be put to death. Along the way, the disciples lead others to Jesus and learn how to live as faithful disciples. At times the journey is successful and exciting; at times they are confused and fear what the future holds.

Near the end of Luke's gospel, after Jesus is resurrected, we read the story of two disciples on a journey to Emmaus (see Luke 24:13–35). As they walk, they encounter a fellow traveler. They do not realize that it is Jesus in their midst. They do not recognize him. He teaches them, both comforting and challenging them. Later as they sit down to eat a meal together, Jesus offers a prayer of thanks. Suddenly they recognize him and as soon as they do, he disappears. They are astonished that he had walked with them all along the road; yet, they did not comprehend his presence!

How has your journey with Jesus changed through the years? Perhaps you were brought up in the church and cannot recall exactly when your journey began. Or, perhaps you remember that very moment when you first made the commitment to follow Jesus. Along the way, you have likely experienced joy and sorrow, calm and strife, sickness and health, success and failure. Perhaps at times it was hard to "keep on keepin' on;" while at other times the journey seemed smooth and easy. Perhaps at times you were keenly aware of Jesus' presence with you, while at other times you felt alone.

Our spiritual journey begins with grace: God's undeserved, unsolicited movement toward us. Our God is graciously predisposed toward us. He wants to be our help in times of need. God yearns to be in a relationship with us. In big and little ways, God moves within our lives to demonstrate his love and care for us. God's grace even precedes our awareness of his presence.

Our journey may feel like aimless wandering until that time when we respond to God's overtures of love shown to us through Christ. Paul tells the Roman Christians, "God proves his love for us in that while we still were sinners Christ died for us" (Romans 5:8). Jesus humbled himself to death on a cross so that we might have the opportunity to enter into relationship with God when we trust in who Jesus is and in what he has done for us. By trusting in Jesus, our sins are forgiven and we receive a companion for our journey: the Holy Spirit. The Holy Spirit makes a home within us and guides us along the way. The Spirit guides and directs us, comforts and corrects us.

So too do we experience the encouragement of fellow travelers, sojourners. The church is a body in motion. We journey together and help one another to stay on course. And that is what we will do together in the weeks to come. Together, we will read and pray, think and discuss, challenge and comfort one another. We'll be invited to open our lives to one another and to the one who calls us to follow. Let the journey begin . . .

Before your group meets together, look at the scripture below and reflect on the questions that follow. You may also wish to journal or make some notes of your thoughts so that you will be able to share them with the other members of your group.

Read Genesis 12:1–9. Abram (whose name was later changed to Abraham) is the father of the Jewish nation. God promises Abram that all the families of the earth will be blessed through him and his descendants. But to receive all the blessings that God promised, Abram had to take the first step of faith and be willing to travel into unfamiliar territory.

Have you ever felt God leading you? Have you ever felt God urging you to change the course of your life and move in a different direction? This goes beyond simply accepting a new job or picking up a new hobby. What I'm speaking of is a change of course, something that may not make any logical sense. Following God is risky business if we take it seriously. *Have you ever felt God calling you to leave your comfort zone and move into unfamiliar territory?*

[Respond in the space below]

Note that, in these verses, Abram twice builds an altar to the Lord. In the Old Testament, the Israelites experienced worship in three different contexts:

1. Fixed times of corporate (group) worship (religious feasts and festivals) that God instructs them to observe regularly (e.g., Passover or the Festival of Booths).

2. Occasional times of worship associated with special events, such as the inauguration of a king or the installation of a high priest. (Keep in mind, Israel was a theocracy—a form of government established and guided by God.)

3. Times of worship by individuals or a small clan to give thanks for, or to lament/confess, events that have personal bearing on their current status. This is reflected in the passage from Genesis.

Worship is—at its core—the giving of praise to God. But worship is also about *encountering* God. It is an encounter with God in a specific time and space: so, Abram constructs an altar, a physical object, to commemorate a particular time and space in which he encounters God.

What connection does this Old Testament story of worship have to our experience of worship today as Christians? How does your church worship experience feel—or not feel—like an encounter with God or an experience of God's presence? Do you feel there are other times, places, and events when you are aware, perhaps even more aware, of encountering God? How does this story impact your understanding of worship?

[Respond in the space below]

The bible writer tells us that Abram journeyed on by stages. *What have been some of the stages in your life's journey?* Turn to the end of this weekly reading and rotate your booklet to a landscape orientation. Draw a line across the top. Now make X's or dots on the paper to identify significant moments on your life's journey. Perhaps it was when you left home to go to college, realizing you would now be responsible for your own decisions. Perhaps it was when your first child was born, realizing you were now responsible for caring for this young life. After "charting" your journey, return to the reflection questions printed below.

How did you experience or encounter God in these significant moments on your life journey? Did any particular one of them especially impact your relationship with God?

[Respond in the space below]

What's the most interesting journey you've ever taken? What made it interesting? Take a picture or souvenir from your journey with you when your group meets and be prepared to share with them a little about your trip.

My Life Journey

Session 2

Scripture: God's Covenant Word

WE ARE RELATIONAL CREATURES. In the second biblical story of creation (beginning at Genesis, chapter 2, verse 4b), our narrator paints a picture of creation "pre-sin." God comes into the garden at the time of the evening breeze (see Genesis 3:8) to walk with the man and woman. What an intimate image! Earlier in chapter 2, the creation of woman is motivated by God's evaluation that "it is not good that the man should be alone" (Gen 2:18). Our God is a relational God who has created us with *an innate desire for relationship*. But healthy relationships need boundaries; they involve expressed expectations and promises. In scripture, the term used to describe relational agreements is *covenant*. Without covenant, we risk (and in fact often realize) chaos and dysfunction in our relationships. Last week, we discussed the covenantal nature of this group. We agreed, mutually, that we would be authentic, respectful, maintain confidentiality, pray for one another, etc. The maintaining of our covenant will help our relationships with one another to deepen and grow over this six-week journey.

Covenants are commitments made in the context of relationship. They define, and often reflect, the nature of the relationship.

Take a moment to reflect on some of the other "covenants" that govern your relationships. Some are very personal and of inestimable value (such as a marriage covenant) while others may seem impersonal and of far less significance (think of a membership at a local gym).

Can you recall a time in your life when, perhaps, you entered into a relationship with someone/s without any stated expectations or boundaries and it created relational ambiguity, ambivalence, or even hostility down the road?

[Respond at the top of the next page]

There are several covenants found in the Old Testament, including:

- God's covenant with Noah (and all humanity) in Genesis 9:8–17.
- God's covenant with Abraham (and his descendants) in Genesis 12:1–3; chapter 15; 17:1–14.
- The Sinai Covenant (often labeled by Christians as "the Ten Commandments") found in Exodus 20 and following, as well as in Deuteronomy 5 and following.
- The Davidic Covenant in 2 Samuel 7:8–17.
- The "New Covenant" in Jeremiah 31:31–34.

As Christians, it is important for us to recognize how the Old Testament covenants defined the relationship between God and Israel. It is also important for us to understand how such Old Testament covenants were interpreted by New Testament authors in relation to the life, death, and resurrection of Jesus.

Paul, in his letter to the Romans, explains that we (followers of Christ Jesus) share in the benefits of God's covenant with Abraham if, like Abraham, we *trust* in the *promises* of God. Paul states that the "goodness" or "right-ness" (righteousness) of Abraham's relationship with God was not because of his ethnicity or even his circumcision. Rather, Abraham was deemed righteous by God (in a right relationship with God) because he *trusted God's promises*. Likewise, we are brought into a right (righteous) relationship with God when we place our trust in the promises of God's salvation through Jesus. Through Paul's interpretation, we are reminded that covenant is, primarily, about a relationship of trust, not mere obedience to rules.

Read through the three scriptures (covenants) listed below:

- Genesis 12:1–3 (Abraham)
- 2 Samuel 7:8–17 (David)
- Jeremiah 31:31–34 (the "New Covenant")

The "New Covenant" proclaimed in Jeremiah is associated by the New Testament authors with Jesus. Through the obedience of Jesus and the gift of the Holy Spirit, we are changed from the inside out; *our hearts are renewed and transformed*. Paul states it this way:

> So if anyone is in Christ, there is a new creation: everything old has passed away; see, everything has become new! All this is from God, who reconciled us to himself through Christ . . . in Christ, God was reconciling the world to himself . . .[12]

Now read Luke 22:14–20. In what we have come to refer to as "the Last Supper," Jesus establishes a new covenant with his disciples. He identifies the bread with his body and the cup with his blood. In the Old Testament, the blood of animals was shed repeatedly in order for sins to be forgiven and the relationship with God to be restored. In the midst of celebrating the Passover meal with his disciples, Jesus redefines the meaning of that meal. He associates it with his impending death (his suffering), but he also associates it with the full and final coming of his kingdom at the end of time. The new covenant celebrated through Holy Communion is a way to remember and honor the saving death of Christ while we await his return.

Because our gospels circulated orally for some time before they were put into written form, our earliest instruction in this new covenant (Holy Communion) is found in Paul's letter to the Corinthians. Read 1 Corinthians 11:17–34. This is a passage of scripture that often results in confusion. When I was young, I remember a woman in my church who never took communion because she was fearful of eating and drinking judgment upon herself (see 1 Corinthians 11:29). But it's important to remember that Paul also employed the metaphor of a human body when speaking of the church. Within the Body of Christ—the Christian Church in Corinth—the wealthy continued to segregate themselves from the poor. "Holy Communion" was celebrated within the context of a church supper. In Corinth, the wealthy began to eat and drink before the poor (who worked long days) had arrived at the meal. The rich gobbled up the best and richest food and wine, and by the time the poorer members arrived, there was little remaining. One can see how such an arrangement could have impacted the health of both the rich (consider diseases like fatty liver, alcoholism or gout) and the poor (inadequate protein or other nutritional deficiencies)![3]

We are relational creatures and our God is a relational God. Jesus came to restore the deep and intimate covenantal relationship that God, from the very beginning of creation, has desired for us. The Bible is not a rule book, a scientific report, or a history book. It is a love story. It reveals across millennia God's ongoing work of healing and restoring our relationships with God and with one another. We know the Word of God in order to know the God of the Word.[4]

---

1. 2 Cor 5:17–19

2. Unless otherwise indicated, all Scripture quotations are from the New Revised Standard Version Bible (NRSV).

3. For a broad discussion of "common" meals as an occasion for segregation by class, see Thiessen, "Social Integration and Sacramental Activity" in *The Social Setting of Pauline Christianity*.

4. Bryant et al., *Companions in Christ*, 79.

Before your group meets together, read through the Ten Commandments as recorded in Deuteronomy 5:1–21. If you attended Sunday School as a child, you may have been encouraged to memorize these commandments. Perhaps there would even be a prize if you could do so!

As you have grown and matured, and in light of this week's reading, reflect on the difference in how you understand or interpret these commandments now. Remembering that healthy and meaningful relationships require boundaries, how might the intent behind these commands be a way to express your love for God and your brothers and sisters in the faith?

[Respond in the space below]

In light of this understanding that obedience to covenantal commands can be an expression of our love for God and our brothers and sisters in the faith, why might Paul have been so adamant—perhaps even disappointed or angry—with the behavior of the Christians in Corinth?

[Respond in the space below]

Are there verses or passages from scripture that you are especially intent on following because you feel they strengthen your relationship with God or others?

[Respond in the space below]

Session 3

Prayer: Fellowship with God

There is a place of quiet rest, near to the heart of God . . .
O Jesus, blest Redeemer, sent from the heart of God,
hold us who wait before thee near to the heart of God.[1]

PRAYER IS THAT WHICH brings us near to the heart of God. Prayer is not talk *about* God or even simply talking *to* God. Prayer is about being in fellowship *with* God through words and silence. Prayer is a natural response to the God who longs to be in relationship with us. Prayer involves a willingness to surrender ourselves to God's purposes and to trust in God's ability to care for us.

There are different types of prayer: praise, confession, thanksgiving, and supplication.

- In prayers of praise, we worship and adore God; we give thanks to God simply for being who God is.

- In confession, we acknowledge our sin and place our trust not only in God's forgiveness, but in the power of God's grace to change, renew, and transform us.

- Thanksgiving springs from our joy and willingness to acknowledge God's gifts and blessings in our lives.

- In supplication, we present our requests before God, including prayers of petition for our own needs and prayers of intercession on behalf of others.

1. McAfee, "Near to the Heart," public domain (also UMC Hymnal, #473).

It is not always easy to pray. Prayer is shaped by our understanding of who God is. If the earliest images and metaphors we were taught caused us to consider God a harsh and impersonal judge, prayer may seem to us a burden or a source of shame.

Furthermore, although prayer involves our being in fellowship with God, we may not always *feel* God's presence. Sometimes in prayer we may feel nothing and wonder if our prayers are getting through. Don't be discouraged by this. Many great saints through the ages have had this same experience. As he teaches his disciples, Jesus reassures us that the heavenly Father knows what we need and is eager to respond to us. In Matthew 6:9–13, Jesus provides a pattern for prayer. (See Appendix A)

Jesus' model prayer begins by acknowledging God's holiness. When we pray, "your kingdom come; your will be done," it is a sort of parallelism. In fact, Jesus assures us that, when we surrender to God's will and purposes, the kingdom of God is made manifest through us. "Daily bread" is symbolic of all of our needs. We are to seek God's provision day by day without unnecessary anxiety about the future (see Matthew 6:25–34).

Furthermore, prayer—no matter how personal it is—is never just about "me and Jesus." We pray with awareness that we are part of God's family, the church; and we recognize that we cannot cultivate our relationship with God without consideration of our relationships with others. So even as we seek God's grace and forgiveness for ourselves, we express our willingness to forgive those who have wronged us. Jesus reminds us, "For if you forgive others their trespasses, your heavenly Father will also forgive you; but if you do not forgive others, neither will your Father forgive your trespasses" (Matthew 6:14–15). Finally, Jesus—who endured the temptations of the devil in the wilderness—teaches us to pray for deliverance, or rescue from the evil one.

At times, prayer may seem difficult or even confusing. Scripture encourages us to approach the throne of grace with boldness (Hebrews 4:16) and to ask, seek, and knock with confidence (Matthew 7:7–8). Meanwhile, we are also reminded that we are to approach God with childlike trust and humility (Matthew 7:9–11). Sometimes holding these two attitudes in balance is what makes prayer both challenging and mysterious.

Ultimately, the practice of prayer deepens our awareness of and responsiveness to God's presence in our lives. As our fellowship with God deepens and expands, we come to understand more fully the words of St. Augustine of Hippo: "You have formed us for yourself [O God], and our hearts are restless 'til they find rest in you."

As you prepare to meet with your group, read through Matthew's version of the Lord's Prayer (Matthew 6:9–13) and Luke's version (Luke 11:2–4). If you are able, read these verses in multiple bible translations or versions. (Different translations of Matthew's version of the prayer are found in Appendix A at the back of your book.)

How do the different translations impact your understanding of the prayer? Do you have a favorite version? Take some time to pray through this prayer slowly, deliberately, and thoughtfully, considering the significance of each phrase as you pray it. If you are accustomed to praying the Lord's Prayer in a group worship setting, how is this prayer experience different?

[Respond in the space below]

As mentioned at the start of this week's reading, prayers of praise are a form of worship. *When you attend weekly worship, do you experience it as a time to praise God for simply being who God is? Based on your experience, do you feel a connection between prayers of praise and congregational worship? Are prayers of praise a regular part of your personal prayer life?*

[Respond in the space below]

Read through Psalm 150. The New Interpreter's Bible Commentary states, "To praise God is to live, and to live is to praise God."[2] With the exception of verse six, each line of the psalm opens with the imperative "praise." The psalm addresses *where* to praise God, *why* God should be praised, (most extensively) *how* God should be praised, and finally, *who* should do the praising. The instruments mentioned in verses 3–5 are instruments associated with ancient Hebrew temple worship.

In twenty-first-century, postmodern, western culture, corporate (or congregational) worship is one of the spiritual practices in greatest decline. *What might be the reason(s) for this? Do you think God desires our praise today, or do you think praise might be a cultural practice that is foreign to our postmodern culture? In our cultural context, who receives public praise and how is the praise expressed?*

[Respond in the space at the top of the next page]

2. McCann, "Psalms," 1279.

Before your group comes together this week, see if you can find an online recording (check on YouTube) of Duke Ellington's setting of Psalm 150 entitled "Praise God and Dance."

Session 4

Generosity: The Cycle of Grace

Every generous act of giving, with every perfect gift, is from above, coming down from the Father of lights, with whom there is no variation or shadow due to change.
James 1:17

I IMAGINE MANY OF us have had the experience of visiting someone with a preschooler in the home. Now, assuming the child is raised by parents who cultivate a secure home environment, the following is a typical scenario:

The child will often ask if you want to see their room. Unlike adults, the child won't worry if their bed is unmade or there are clothes on the floor. Upon entering their room, the child will proceed to point out all of her/his favorite belongings and, quite likely, will offer something to you. In the midst of your "tour," they may take back some items, but will leave others in your care. It will not cross their mind to consider how much the possession may have cost or whether it can be replaced. It is something that brings them joy and so, spontaneously, they want to share that joy with you. Before you leave your friend's home, you'll need to empty out your pockets—although there will, likely, be something you will decide to take with you because the opportunity to give is important to the child. Children are naturally generous.

In Luke, chapter 12, Jesus is asked to arbitrate a dispute between two brothers over their inheritance. In response, Jesus tells a parable. The parable is about a rich landowner. He is fortunate to have an abundant harvest—so large, in fact, that his barns cannot contain it. But he is loath to share his good fortune with others, so he tears down his barns and builds bigger barns to accommodate this bounty. The rich man hoards his wealth because he seeks security and ease for his future. He says to himself, "You have ample goods laid up for many years; relax, eat, drink and be merry"

(Luke 12:19). But the rich man is in for a surprise: that very night he dies and, as they say, "you can't take it with you."

Read the parable of the rich fool in Luke 12:13–20. This parable is a story about stewardship and it is also a story about relationships. In the culture of Jesus' day, those with great wealth were considered blessed by God; but they were blessed in order to be a blessing to others. First-century Palestinian culture was a patron-benefactor culture. The wealthy were expected to function as patrons by providing for the needs of the poor, their "clients." The poor, in turn, would "pay back" their patron by publicly praising them: by telling others about their generosity. This public praise would boost the honor or reputation of their benefactor. Think of it as the "thank you note" of the ancient world! All this was a beautiful cycle of gracious giving.

Here is a more extensive explanation of the "Three Graces" in the first-century Mediterranean world:[1]

- Grace was used to describe the generous *disposition* of a patron toward their client. (This is often how we think of grace—i.e., God is predisposed to show us mercy.)

- Grace was used to describe the *gift or help* that was given to the client by their patron. (Think of the forgiveness and eternal life we receive as a manifestation of grace from God through Jesus.)

- Grace referred to the *gratitude* expressed by the client in response to the gift. (We might call this "Christian commitment" or "living for Jesus.")

In what ways does your lifestyle (the way in which you live) demonstrate gratitude to God for the gift of eternal life through Jesus? [Respond in the space below]

The parable of the rich fool would further seem to imply that how we manage our blessings or resources is not something personal or private. It has implications for our relationship with God, other people, and all of creation.

In your life, has there ever been a time when you realized or recognized that you had been accumulating to excess a resource someone else needed? Conversely, when have

---

1. For additional information on this topic, see: DeSilva, "Grace" in the *Eerdmans Dictionary of the Bible*, 525, as well as DeSilva, *An Introduction to the New Testament, 2nd ed., 100–108*. For a more in-depth discussion see, DeSilva, *Honor, Patronage, Kinship, and Purity*, 132–37.

you been able to release or surrender a resource that was precious to you when you recognized it could be a much-needed blessing to someone else?

[Respond in the space below]

The parable of the rich fool also raises a question of trust or faith. Without a firmly established trust (or faith) in God's grace, we will foolishly seek security from the things of this world just as the rich fool did. Although we don't often acknowledge it, the teaching of this parable is at odds with twenty-first-century Western capitalist culture. Think about it. We are told that we must save our money and invest it wisely or we will suffer the ultimate and horrible fate: outliving our money! But, implicit in the power of this contemporary cultural admonition is the assumption that money can and will secure our futures. *The message of the parable is that it cannot.*

In Mark, chapter 10, Jesus is approached by a wealthy man seeking to *inherit* eternal life. His choice of words is interesting, isn't it? The exchange between Jesus and the man comes to an abrupt end when Jesus tells him that he should "go, sell what you own, and give the money to the poor, and you will have treasure *in heaven*; then come, follow me" (Mark 10:21b, emphasis mine). This is more than the man can bear; he "went away grieving for he had many possessions" (Mark 10:22b). We are not told the precise reason for his grief and there is always some danger in "psychologizing" biblical characters, but it seems the man recognizes his own inability to choose between the benefits of money in this life or the blessing of eternal life in the presence of God.

Think about your own attitude toward security. *From whom or what do you seek security? Do you believe that we can ever live truly generous lives if we are plagued by fear and insecurity? How might fear and insecurity throw a monkey wrench into the cycle of grace?*

[Respond in the space below]

In most churches, individuals are not compelled to disclose their financial position and assets. We treat it as a private matter.

But, if you were truly honest with yourself and God, are you as generous as you'd like to be? If you practice tithing (giving 10% of your income) or percentage giving in general, do you factor the percentage based on your gross or your net income? Is your giving based solely on your paycheck or do you give based on all of your income sources, such as interest, stock dividends, the holiday bonus, etc.?

[Respond in the space below]

Do you practice "prejudicial giving," e.g., you are generous when funding the youth mission trip but far more frugal when contributing to the church (or other nonprofits') operating expenses?

[Respond in the space below]

Finally, how does your giving reflect your covenantal commitment to Christ and to your Christian brothers and sisters?

[Respond in the space below]

It is sometimes difficult to take a risk and trust in the faithful generosity of God. But we can depend upon the words of our Lord found in Matthew 6:25–33:

> *Therefore I tell you, do not worry about your life, what you will eat or what you will drink, or about your body, what you will wear . . . Study the birds of the air; they neither sow nor reap nor gather into barns, and yet your heavenly Father feeds them. Are you not of more value than they? . . . Examine the lilies of the*

field . . . they neither toil nor spin, yet I tell you, even Solomon in all his glory was not clothed like one of these . . . Therefore, do not worry . . . For it is the Gentiles who strive for all these things; and indeed your heavenly Father knows that you need all these things. But strive first for the kingdom of God and his righteousness, and all these things will be given to you as well.

Was this week's reading what you expected? Did it influence your understanding of generosity and the correlation between trust in Jesus and the ability to be generous with others? Did this week's reading introduce questions you'd not previously considered?

[Respond in the space below]

Session 5

Evangelism: Sharing Our Stories

I HAVE A FRIEND, Tim, who was born and raised in the Memphis, Tennessee area. No one can tell a story like Tim and many of his stories relate to events and happenings in his hometown. People from Tim's church and his community "come to life" as you listen to his stories.

Cultures have always recorded their history through the telling of stories. With the exception of some Hebrew writings (e.g., Psalms and Proverbs) or the letters (or epistles) found in the New Testament, nearly all of our scripture began as oral history or stories. Perhaps you can envision ancient people sitting around a fire hearing stories of patriarchs like Abraham, Isaac and Jacob, or stories of kings like David and Solomon.

Stories help us understand who we are and where we come from. They help us identify how God is working in our life. I come from a small, predominantly blue-collar Appalachian city. My father dropped out of school in the eighth grade so he could work and help support his family. He became a Christian as an adult and, in his thirties, felt a call into ministry. He secured his GED, enrolled in college, and subsequently seminary. Decades later, as I look back over *my* life, I realize how different it might have been had my dad not pursued higher education and responded to God's call.

Richard Peace, in his book *Spiritual Journaling*, writes of "hinges:" turning points in our lives that move us in a new direction or yield particular insight.[1] During our first week together, you were encouraged to reflect on your life's journey and to identify significant moments along the way. These are what Peace might describe as "hinge" events.

1. Peace, *Spiritual Journaling*, 34.

As people of faith, knowing our history and being aware of the significant chang-
es that take place in our lives provides the opportunity for us to view our individual
stories, circumstances, and events through the lens of faith in order to discern the
ways and places that God's Spirit is leading, guiding, and equipping us. We want to
live with *spiritual self-awareness*, taking time periodically to consider, remember, and
evaluate our lives and how God is at work in our lives. Sister Irene Nowell writes:
"telling our stories leads us to understand who we are . . . If our stories are not told, the
depth of our souls will not be known."[2]

Did you know there is a genre of literature called *spiritual autobiographies*? Augustine of Hippo may have written the first spiritual autobiography, entitled *Confes-
sions*. If we utilize journaling as a spiritual discipline (recording not only events and
happenings, but also our inward feelings and growth), then journaling can become
the venue through which our spiritual autobiographies unfold over time. The journals
of John Wesley, the founder of the Methodist movement, function as a spiritual autobiography as, within them, Wesley identifies the struggles and growth in his relationship with God through Christ and in his relationships with fellow Christians. In his
journal he writes of what has become a famous spiritual "mountain top experience" (a
significant moment or "hinge-point") when, on May 24, 1738, he attended a meeting
on Aldersgate Street where someone was reading from Martin Luther's *Preface to the
Romans*. Later in his journal, Wesley wrote,

> while he was describing the change which God works in the heart through faith
> in Christ, I felt my heart strangely warmed. I felt I did trust in Christ, Christ
> alone for salvation; and an assurance was given me that He had taken away my
> sins, even mine, and saved me from the law of sin and death.[3]

This event was neither the beginning nor the end of Wesley's spiritual journey.
However, Wesley identified this experience as crucial to his faith development.

Lisa Hess, in her book *Artisanal Theology*, writes,

> You know less about yourself now than you will when you have shared your
> story. If you are willing to risk becoming more aware of the mystery of being
> human and a child of God, you will come to hear unexpected elements of your
> own story . . . [4]

This week, we will practice writing (or sketching) our own spiritual autobiographies. Think of it as a way to put your spiritual journey into words or pictures. As
you take time to write your spiritual autobiography—to put your journey down on
paper—you may discover more about yourself. You may become more aware of God's
movement in your life. You may notice connections of which you were previously

2. Nowell, *Pleading, Cursing, Praising*, 11.

3. Outler, *John Wesley*, 66.

4. Hess, *Artisanal Theology*, 111.

unaware. It is important to write or draw out your autobiography and not simply think about it. The very act of writing or putting something on paper helps to crystallize and organize our thoughts.

This week will be a different experience when you come together with your group. Rather than discussing the reading and engaging in some group practices or exercises, you will be invited to share *a portion* of your spiritual autobiography with your group.

Refer back to week one and the significant moments you noted along the time-line of your life's journey. Richard Peace recommends dividing your life into a series of time periods that are bookended by these significant moments or transitions.

These could be things like:[5]

- Moving to a different state;

- Getting married or divorced;

- Going off to college;

- Having your first child;

- A career change

Once you have blocked out the time periods, Peace further encourages noting how periods of our lives are influenced or impacted by:

- Key people and relationships;

- Primary activities, responsibilities or roles;

- Any strong emotions you recall;

- National or global events that impacted you;

- Personal health;

- Creative impulses, dreams or ideas that developed during this time;

- Significant spiritual events and your relationship with God during this period

What is listed above is a suggestion, but you may develop your spiritual auto-biography in whatever format best allows you to identify God's movement in your life. Remember that a spiritual autobiography is not the same as a diary. The goal is not to compile a chronological listing of events and activities. A good length for your spiritual autobiography is 4–5 pages. Pray before you begin, asking the Spirit to reveal to you the significant landmarks along your spiritual journey.

You may feel some trepidation about sharing your story with the others in your group. You will be asked to share *only one* time period (1–2 pages). You may select what you feel most comfortable sharing. Your group leader will share first to "demystify"

---

5. Some content taken from *Spiritual Journaling*, by Richard Peace. Copyright © 1995. Used by permission of NavPress. All rights reserved. Represented by Tyndale House Publishers, Inc. www.tyndale.com. Peace, *Spiritual Journaling*, 36–7.

the experience. Remember that we are on this journey together and sharing our stories allows us to encourage and guide one another. Be sincere and trust that the Holy Spirit will work within your group as you open your hearts and lives to one another.

Subsequent pages have been left blank to write or sketch your spiritual autobiography within this booklet.

Spiritual Autobiography

Session 6

Service: Finding Our Role in the Church and the World

THE CHURCH IS THE body of Christ given for the world. In other words, the church does not exist for itself. Some have said the church is the only institution that exists for non-members! Certainly, the church is a place where members should be able to count on encouragement in the face of life's challenges and support in their Christian discipleship. But ultimately, the role of the church is to be the presence of Christ in and for the world.

So how, exactly, do we do that? We do that by utilizing our God-given gifts to further the mission of Christ. This process begins with our willingness and commitment to be available wherever and however God needs us. Sometimes our interest in spiritual gifts can become narcissistic as we become so focused on our individual gifts that we are unwilling to do anything that does not allow us to showcase them. Certainly, we are gifted in unique and special ways. But we must be willing to be used by God in whatever way the Holy Spirit guides us.

In the gospel of Mark (chapter 1, verses 16–20), we read of Jesus calling his first disciples, who were fishermen. Mark tells us that they responded to Jesus' call *with immediacy*:

> *As Jesus passed along the Sea of Galilee, he saw Simon and his brother Andrew casting a net into the sea— for they were fishermen. And Jesus said to them, "Follow me and I will make you fish for people." And immediately, they left their nets and followed him. As he went a little farther, he saw James son of Zebedee and his brother John, who were in their boat mending the nets. Immediately he called them; and they left their father Zebedee in the boat with the hired men, and followed him.*

God places a call upon all of our lives. If we are willing to make ourselves radically available to God, God will use us. As we offer ourselves to Christ, his Holy Spirit moves within us: guiding us, directing us, and equipping us. On our own, by our own strength and abilities, we could not hope to discern and fulfill God's call; but it is the Spirit of Christ within us who accomplishes this work.

This guidance of the Holy Spirit within us is demonstrated in the sacrament of baptism. In the early Church, people were often baptized by immersion. It was a powerful symbol, revealing that, by offering our lives to Christ, we desire our sinfulness and selfishness to be "drowned to death" so that the loving and life-giving Spirit of Christ may "rise up" within us. The apostle Paul wrote to the Christians in Rome:

> *Do you not know that all of us who have been baptized into Christ Jesus were baptized into his death? Therefore we have been buried with him by baptism into death, so that, just as Christ was raised from the dead by the glory of the Father, so we too might walk in newness of life . . . So you also must consider yourselves dead to sin and alive to God in Christ Jesus.* (Romans 6:3–4, 11)

How do we become people who can be radically used by God to accomplish God's work in the world? We do this by allowing the Holy Spirit to put to death our ego and pride that cause us to serve for our own glory or satisfaction, or only to respond when it is convenient. It is the work of the Spirit to lead us into a new way of living that reflects Jesus' servant ministry and is a demonstration of God's love and grace.

Yet even so, we do acknowledge and celebrate that each of us, created uniquely in the image of God, has been given distinctive gifts with which to serve. These are known as *spiritual gifts*. The apostle Paul speaks of these gifts often in his letters to his churches.[1] We should not consider Paul's lists as exhaustive. Paul wrote about the gifts both evident and necessary within those first-century Christian communities. In our twenty-first-century world, some of those gifts are still much needed and, therefore, undoubtedly still bestowed upon believers. However, there may be other gifts needed for our cultural context today which the Spirit also gives in order to carry out God's mission in our current time and place.

So, how do we go about discerning and discovering our spiritual gifts? One way is to exercise self-awareness. If we discipline ourselves to take time periodically to prayerfully reflect on our lives, we can better discern God's call. Our life's *experiences* are used by God to shape us and guide us.

A second way to discern our gifts is to receive affirmation or confirmation from fellow believers. Our *relationships* are also used by God to shape us and guide us. In particular, brothers and sisters in Christ (like the ones in this group) who are willing to listen, to pray, and to respond with truth and love can serve as spiritual guides.

Sometimes exercising our spiritual gifts fits nicely into our lives and requires little change to our normal routine. But, at other times, exercising a spiritual gift may

---

1. For examples, see Romans 12:3–8; Ephesians 4:1–6, 11–13; 1 Corinthians 12:4–11, 27–31.

disrupt our life as we know it and may even require personal sacrifice. Yet, either way, we will discover that answering God's call and exercising our spiritual gifts allows us to participate in the mission of Christ to bring about redemption for God's world.

Before your group meets together, take some time this week to evaluate your past in order to better discern God's call upon your future. Richard Peace writes: *"For the follower of Christ, it is important to become what God wants us to become . . . One way to discern God's future for you is to pay attention to the past."*[2]

Using the blank space below each question, write some notes about your past by considering:[3]

What particular *talents* do you have? In what areas have you demonstrated proficiency and been affirmed by others? [Respond in the space below]

In what ways have you volunteered or *served* to meet the needs of others? What experience/s did you find *especially gratifying*? [Respond in the space below]

In your work, in your play, in your relationships and experiences, what has been the greatest source/s of *delight* to you? What is it that consistently energizes you? [Respond at the top of the next page]

2. Peace, *Spiritual Journaling*, 54.

3. Some content taken from *Spiritual Journaling*, by Richard Peace. Copyright © 1995. Used by permission of NavPress. All rights reserved. Represented by Tyndale House Publishers, Inc. www.tyndale.com.

What *need* draws your attention and causes great compassion to well up within you? [Respond in the space below]

Leader Guide

Session 1

(ITEMS NEEDED: A CANDLE and small stones. You will need a stone for each member of your group. These small stones can be collected outside or purchased at a craft store.)

Explain what the group format will be each session:

- Light a candle

- Hear a word of scripture

- Take a few moments to breathe deeply and relax

- Have a time of prayer that will conclude with the Lord's Prayer

As you begin, light a candle and explain that it is a reminder to us of Jesus' presence with us since Jesus is the light of the world. Read this scripture from Psalm 139:1–3:

> O Lord, you have searched me and known me. You know when I sit down and when I rise up; you discern my thoughts from far away. You search out my path and my lying down, and are acquainted with all my ways.

Invite members to take a few moments to close their eyes and breathe deeply and slowly, using these moments to begin to relax and let go of the day's tensions.

[Note: For people unacquainted with practicing silence, even a minute can feel like an eternity. You may want to begin with a period as short as 90 seconds and gradually increase your time of silence each week. However, it is recommended that the time of silence not be eliminated. The practice of silence is a spiritual discipline that is widely neglected in our culture.]

Explain to the group that you will open with prayer. They can then name anyone or any situation for which they desire prayer. All they need to do is speak the name of the one in need, since God already knows every need. Let them know that the prayer time will conclude with the Lord's Prayer.

[Note: Unless you are confident that *all* participants know the prayer by memory, it is wise to refer them to Appendix A and select the version that the group will pray together. Keep in mind that some contemporary services do not include the Lord's Prayer, so even church attendees may not be familiar with it.]

Explain to group participants what this group will be like . . .

We're entering into relationship not only with Jesus, but with one another. Together, we'll focus more on *formation* and *discovery* than on *information* and *answers*. We will do so through weekly readings and reflections, as well as group sharing and conversation.

Our group will be in covenant with one another. A covenant is an agreement that defines *how* we'll be in relationship with each another. Explain to group members that next week's reading and reflection will examine the meaning of covenant more deeply.

So that this group is a safe and meaningful experience, we'll need to be in covenant with one another. Invite participants to turn to the covenant printed in Appendix C. Have members of the group take turns reading the bullet points on their covenant. After doing so, ask if they feel comfortable with, and are willing to commit to, the conditions of this covenant.

During the week, group members were invited to reflect on the most interesting trip or journey they've ever taken. Invite members to introduce themselves by saying their name and talking about the most interesting journey they've ever taken. Some may have pictures or souvenirs. (Obviously, if members of the group all know one another, introductions will not be necessary.) Encourage participants to share what made the journey so interesting. In particular, be attentive to noticing if individuals had companions on this journey and how that made their journey more meaningful. Listen to notice if there were parts of the journey that were especially surprising, beautiful, anxiety-producing, etc. After everyone has shared, take a few moments to summarize some of what you heard as it relates to the items listed above (journey companions, surprises, beauty, anxiety, etc.). Ask group members if they heard any connections among their experiences (e.g., shared experiences).

Share briefly something about your own journey of faith. Who has companioned you on your faith journey? What have been some of the most surprising, beautiful, and anxious moments along the way?

Read the scripture for this week, Genesis 12:1–9. Point out some key points in the story:

- In order for Abram to receive the blessing God promised, he had to step out in faith, leaving his current home to go to a new and unfamiliar place.

- Abram was old and he and his wife had never been able to conceive. They had no children and yet God makes a promise that is for Abram's descendants ("To your offspring I will give this land" – Gen 12:7)!

- Abram responds to God's promise of blessing by *worshiping* God (he builds an altar and invokes God's name).

Invite group members to respond to the reflection questions below:

- Have they ever felt God leading them? Have they ever felt God urging them to change the course of their life and move in a different direction?

- Have they ever felt God calling them to step out of their comfort zone and move into unfamiliar territory?

- In our day and age, does God still speak to us? Does it seem right or practical that God would invite us to take a risk in order to receive blessings God has prepared for us?

Abram built an altar to mark the place where he had encountered God. Worship, at its core, is about encountering God. In worship, we encounter God in a particular time and space. Ask:

- How does the story of Abram impact your understanding of worship?

- If you attend weekly corporate worship, do you feel like it is an encounter with God? Are there other times, places, and events where you are more aware of God's presence?

- As twenty-first-century western Christians, how might we appropriately mark or distinguish those times, places, and experiences of encountering God's presence?

During the week, group members were asked to "chart" significant moments on their life journeys by drawing a line and marking these moments. Invite participants to turn back to the chart from week 1 and to share a couple of those significant moments. Invite them to share how those moments impacted their relationship with God. Let group members know that—later in our journey together—they will be asked to share more of their spiritual journeys with one another. Encourage them to continue to reflect on the significant moments they identified on the chart this week.

Read Mark 1:16–20. When Jesus called his first disciples, they immediately dropped their nets and followed him without really knowing where it was that they were headed. Ask participants:

- Have they ever encountered or experienced something so compelling that it warranted an immediate change/response in their life?

- What might it have been about Jesus and his call that caused these fishermen to respond immediately, without hesitation?

Invite participants to close their eyes as you read these verses of Mark again and to imagine themselves in the story. Invite them to imagine that Jesus is calling them to drop whatever it is in their life that defines them. Encourage them to consider what it might feel like to drop everything for Jesus. What would be hardest for them to release: a prized possession, an important relationship, a role or a job that may define them?

In the Old Testament, at various times, God's people would erect stones as altars in places where they had encountered God in real and life-changing ways. Pass out a small stone to participants. Encourage them to place the stone somewhere in their home or workplace where they will see it frequently and allow it to remind them that God is stirring and moving within their lives and inviting them to follow wherever God may lead.

Extinguish the candle you lit at the beginning of this session.

End with a prayer of blessing from Numbers 6:24–26:

> The Lord bless you and keep you; the Lord make his face to shine upon you, and be gracious to you; the Lord lift up his countenance upon you, and give you peace. Amen.

Session 2

(ITEMS NEEDED: A CANDLE and a bible. Although this is not designed to be an in-depth bible study, as the facilitator, you may wish to have a bible dictionary with you for quick reference for questions that may come up. See the list of resources at the conclusion of this session for recommendations.)

Begin by reviewing the group covenant by asking a participant to read through the covenant (provided in Appendix C).

Remind the group of the format for each session:

- Light a candle

- Hear a word of scripture

- Take a few moments to breathe deeply and relax

- Have a time of prayer that will conclude with the Lord's Prayer

Light the candle and explain that it is a reminder to us of Jesus' presence with us since Jesus is the light of the world. Read this scripture from Psalm 119:105: *"Your word, [O Lord,] is a lamp to my feet and a light to my path."*

Invite members to take a few moments to close their eyes and breathe deeply and slowly, using these moments to begin to relax and let go of the day's tensions.

Invite group members to name anyone or any situation for which they desire prayer. All they need to do is speak the name of the one in need, since God already knows every need. Let them know that the prayer time will conclude with the Lord's Prayer. (Reference Appendix A)

Ask group members:

- Prior to this week, how familiar were you with the concept of covenant?

- Through your reading, did you reflect on the covenantal nature of any of the relationships in your life? Outside of scripture, what covenant/s is/are most important to you in your life?

- Were all of the covenants in this week's reading ones that you were already familiar with? If not, what did you learn?

- Near the end of this week's reading, it was stated "The bible is not a rule book, a scientific report, or a history book. It is a love story . . . " What do you think of that statement? Can we consider the bible true without applying our postmodern scientific or historical standards for truth? If you believe the bible to be true, what do you mean when you make that affirmation?

- This week we read from Paul's letter to the Corinthians (1 Cor 11:17–34). In this passage of scripture, Paul addresses how the Corinthian Christians are putting the new covenant, the Lord's Supper, into practice. In verse 20, Paul tells them, "When you come together, it is not really to eat the Lord's Supper." Why is Paul critical of the Corinthians? How is the behavior of the Corinthians undermining the integrity of covenant?

- You were asked to reflect on how you now understand the Ten Commandments as an adult, and in light of this week's reading. Remembering that healthy and meaningful relationships require boundaries, how might the intent behind these commands be a way to express your love for God and others? What biblical commands or mandates do you follow expressly because you feel they strengthen your relationship with God and with other people?

Genesis 1 is a very organized presentation of creation. It may have even been used like a worship liturgy (note the repeating phrases/patterns that may have been congregational responses). Genesis 2 has a much more "earthy" feel and is likely the older of the two stories.

Invite the group to listen as you read Genesis 2:4b–9; 15–23; and 3:1–13. Then ask:

- What does this story teach us about the nature of God?

- What does it teach us about human nature?

- What does it teach us about the relationship God wants to have with us?

Now invite the group to listen as you read the parable of the Prodigal Son in Luke 15:11–32. Read it through twice. On the first reading, ask group members to imagine themselves as the younger son: that is, placing themselves in the story as that son. On the second reading, invite them to imagine themselves as the eldest son, placing themselves within the story as that son. Then ask:

- How do we hear the parable differently from the two points of view?

- How is this parable a story about covenant?

- What does it tell us about God's relationship with us?

- What does it teach us about how we are to respond to those who have "gone astray?"

- In ancient Palestinian culture, it was assumed and understood that the eldest son would assist his father in carrying out the duties of hospitality. By refusing to even join in the celebration, this eldest son also dishonors his father. Has there ever been an occasion when you recognized that your judgment of someone dishonored Christ and his gift of grace?

Extinguish the candle you lit at the beginning of this session. End with a prayer of blessing from Numbers 6:24–26:

> *The Lord bless you and keep you; the Lord make his face to shine upon you, and be gracious to you; the Lord lift up his countenance upon you, and give you peace.* Amen.

List of Resources for Biblical Study and Interpretation:

Donohue, John R. "Guidelines for Reading and Interpretation" In *The New Interpreter's Study Bible*, 2261–67. Nashville: Abingdon, 2003.

Freedman, David Noel, et al., eds. *Eerdmans Dictionary of the Bible*. Grand Rapids: Eerdmans, 2000.

Gaventa, Beverly Roberts, and David Petersen, eds. *The New Interpreter's Bible: One Volume Commentary*. Nashville: Abingdon, 2010.

Harrelson, Walter J., ed. *The New Interpreter's Study Bible: New Revised Standard Version with the Apocrypha*. Rev. ed. Nashville: Abingdon, 2003.

Powell, Mark Allan, ed. *The HarperCollins Bible Dictionary (Revised and Updated)*. New York: HarperCollins, 2011.

Session 3

(ITEMS NEEDED: A CANDLE and a bible. Note that Appendix B will be used in this session but should not be referenced until the conclusion of the session.)

Review the group covenant by inviting a participant to read through the covenant (printed in Appendix C).

Remind the group of the format for each session:

- Light a candle
- Hear a word of scripture
- Take a few moments to breathe deeply and relax
- Have a time of prayer that will conclude with the Lord's Prayer

Light the candle and explain that it is a reminder of Jesus' presence with us since Jesus is the light of the world. Read this scripture based on Psalm 19:14: *As we gather as your people in this time and in this space, O God, may the words of our mouths and the meditations of our hearts be acceptable to you, O Lord, our rock and our redeemer. Amen.*

Invite members to take a few moments to close their eyes and breathe deeply and slowly, using these moments to begin to relax and let go of the day's tensions.

Invite group members to name anyone or any situation for which they desire prayer. All they need to do is speak the name of the one in need, since God already knows every need. Let them know that the prayer time will conclude with the Lord's Prayer. (Reference Appendix A)

Review with the group the different types of prayers they read about this week: praise, thanksgiving, confession, and supplication. Talk with them to be sure they understand the differences between these types of prayers. Ask group members if they learned anything new about prayer through their reading this week.

In particular, ask participants to share what they believe is the difference between prayers of praise and prayers of thanksgiving. Explain that Eastern culture (in ancient times and today) is a communal culture. People think of themselves not in individualistic terms, but as part of a group—their extended family, their village, etc. This way of thinking is reflected in biblical psalms of praise by utilizing first person *plural* pronouns. Likewise, in the Book of Common Prayer and other Christian prayer books, prayers are corporate in nature. We are encouraged to pray in 1st person plural, even in our personal prayer time. Ask them to consider: *what might be the value in this kind of communal/collective prayer?*

Inquire how they liked the experience of praying the Lord's Prayer in different versions. Was there a particular translation they liked best? If so, why? How did their experience with the Lord's Prayer (on their own) this week differ from any previous experiences of praying the Lord's Prayer (with others) during a worship service (congregational worship)?

Share with the group that there are many different ways of praying. We can pray by meditating and making use of a visual object (such as a cross) or a single word (such as "peace") used as a mantra. As our reading emphasized, prayer is about sharing fellowship with God and being attentive to God's presence. Prayer is about developing our relationship with God. More than a list of things we want from God for ourselves and others, *prayer gets to the heart of discerning what it is we are seeking in a relationship with Christ.*

Invite the group to listen as you read the following scripture from the gospel of John (chapter 1, verses 35–39):

> *The next day John again was standing with two of his disciples, and as he watched Jesus walk by, he exclaimed, "Look, here is the Lamb of God!" The two disciples heard him say this, and they followed Jesus. When Jesus turned and saw them following, he said to them, "What are you looking for?" They said to him, "Rabbi" (which translated means Teacher), "where are you staying?" He said to them, "Come and see." They came and saw where he was staying, and they remained with him that day. It was about four o'clock in the afternoon.*

Remind participants that, as we pray, we express to God that which we are truly seeking in our lives: the deepest longings of our hearts. Prayer is a dialogue. Through prayer, God asks us now (as Jesus asked his followers long ago), "What are you looking for?"

One very ancient form of prayer that helped people be attentive to God's presence was breath prayer. Breath prayer is a way to "practice the presence of God." Many people use scripture, hymns, or choruses to fashion their breath prayer. It is something we can repeat (aloud or silently) to focus us in our prayer time, and we can repeat it through the day to keep our attention focused on God. A breath prayer is something we can use every day, even when we are rushed and short on time. A breath prayer is as unique as our lives and our relationship with God.

Let the group know that you will lead them through an exercise to begin to develop their own unique breath prayer.[1] [At the conclusion of the session, point out the breath prayer pattern in Appendix B, *but do not call attention to it now or they will be distracted by reading instructions,* rather than listening and experiencing the process.]

- Step 1: Close your eyes and focus on your breathing

[Allow some time here for quiet]

- Step 2: Imagine God is calling you by name. God is asking of you as Jesus asked of his disciples long ago, "What are you looking for? What are you seeking?"

[Invite them to take a moment to reflect on this question]

- Step 3: Respond to God with what it is that you are seeking; express to God the deepest longings of your heart.

[Allow additional time for reflection]

- Step 4: Think of the various names or titles for God: Lord, Mighty God, Good Shepherd, Savior, Advocate, etc. Choose the name or title that means the most to you.

[Allow time for reflection]

- Step 5: Now, combine the name and what you are seeking into one phrase, e.g., "Good Shepherd, lead and guide me."

[Allow time for reflection]

Invite participants to share (if they so desire) what this breath prayer experience was like for them; inquire if they have any questions about the process of developing a personal breath prayer.

Invite group members to share aloud occasions or experiences in their lives that have made it difficult for them to pray. What obstacles or impediments to prayer have they experienced? (Allow time for response and discussion.)

One impediment to prayer can be our own reluctance to give up control. Prayer is an act of trust and submission to God and God's purposes. Quaker pastor and author, Richard Foster, discusses submission as a spiritual discipline. When we pray "Thy will be done," we are submitting to God and God's purposes for our lives and in our world. Foster teaches that there can be great freedom and liberty in submission. Prayer is, ultimately, an expression of submission, "the ability to lay down the terrible burden of always needing to get our own way."[2]

---

1. The form presented here has been adapted from Barton, *Sacred Rhythms*, 76.
2. Foster, *Celebration of Discipline*, 111.

Invite group members to share: *have there been times in their lives when they have struggled to trust God and to submit to God?*

Along with better knowing God, prayer also helps us know ourselves better. It helps us understand what our inward desires and motivations are. It helps us put our thoughts and actions into clearer perspective. One ancient form of prayer was called the Prayer of Examen. This form of prayer, developed by Saint Ignatius, is a wonderful way to tune in and assess our lives on a daily basis. It is a particularly helpful way to conclude our day before we go to sleep. Lead the group in this abbreviated form of Ignatius' Prayer of Examen:[3] (At the conclusion of this session, point out that this prayer pattern, as well, can be found in Appendix B.)

Invite group members to close their eyes and take a moment to consider:

- *Gift*: What gifts have you received or given to others over the course of this day (or week); in other words, when did you demonstrate love or kindness toward another, and when did you receive love or kindness from someone else?

[allow quiet time for reflection]

- *Struggle*: Over the past day (or week), recall a time or times when you failed to give and receive love; recall times when you may have felt anxious or resentful about unresolved issues.

[allow quiet time for reflection]

- *Invitation*: Now consider, what gift or kindness would you seek from God in order to move forward in an attitude of peace and wholeness? What, among God's many mercies (things like forgiveness, strength, peace, courage), do you most need from God today? Reflect on this as you breathe slowly and rest in God's grace.

[allow quiet time for reflection]

Invite group members to reflect upon this prayer experience and encourage them to share any final thoughts, questions, or concerns they have around the topic of prayer.

Close your time together by letting members know that our scriptures also contain prayers of blessing, a type of intercessory prayer. Now, call attention to Appendix B and the Prayer of Blessing. Ask members to read this Prayer of Blessing together aloud as a prayer on behalf of one another.

Extinguish the candle and bid them God's peace, saying "peace be with you" as you part.

---

3. This abbreviated form of the Prayer of Examen is based on an adaptation found in Brown, *Paths to Prayer*, 87. The prayer has been adapted with the author's consent.

Session 4

(Items needed: candle and Bible)

Review the group covenant by inviting a participant to read the covenant aloud (printed in Appendix C).

Remind the group of the format for each session:

- Light a candle

- Hear a word of scripture

- Take a few moments to breathe deeply and relax

- Have a time of prayer that will conclude with the Lord's Prayer

Light the candle and explain that it is a reminder to us of Jesus' presence with us, since Jesus is the light of the world. Read the scriptures below from James and John:

> James 1:17: *Every generous act of giving, with every perfect gift, is from above, coming down from the Father of lights, with whom there is no variation or shadow due to change.*

> John 3:16 *For God so loved the world that he gave his only Son, so that everyone who believes in him may not perish but may have eternal life.*

Invite members to take a few moments to close their eyes and breathe deeply and slowly, using the time to begin to relax and let go of the day's tensions.

Invite group members to name anyone or any situation for which they desire prayer. All they need to do is speak the name of the one in need, since God already knows every need. Let them know that the prayer time will conclude with the Lord's Prayer (reference Appendix A).

Invite participants to discuss and respond to the questions below:

- *What is the best gift you've ever received? What made it a good gift?*

- *What do "gifts" reveal with regard to relationships? Has a gift you've been given ever impacted your relationship with someone, perhaps even changed your feelings toward them?*

- *When you hear the word "gift," what comes to mind? Something tangible or intangible?*

This week's reading focused on the spiritual practice of generosity. If you attend church, you may be more accustomed to the term "stewardship." Stewardship typically relates to the way in which we manage our resources, but stewardship is also *relational*. That's why this week's reading used the term "generosity." Generosity is a more easily recognized *relational* term. Whether we are conscious of it or not, how we manage our resources reveals and impacts the nature of our relationship with God and with others.

In the New Testament, the Greek word we interpret as "believe" is *pisteuo*. A more accurate translation of the word would be "to trust" or "to have confidence."

When we hear the words "believe" and "trust" in English, are they always interchangeable? What different impressions might they leave us with? [Give the group time to reflect and respond.]

"Trust" is a relational term as well. Jesus, in his parables and other teachings, makes clear that we cannot place our trust in God *and* in money. Like a lover; we can only fully give our heart to one.

Invite the group to listen as you read this story from Mark 10:17–22 of a rich man who seeks eternal life:

> *As Jesus was setting out on a journey, a man ran up and knelt before him, and asked him, "Good Teacher, what must I do to inherit eternal life?" Jesus said to him . . . "You know the commandments: 'You shall not murder; you shall not commit adultery; you shall not steal; you shall not bear false witness; you shall not defraud; honor your father and mother.'" He said to Jesus, "Teacher, I have kept all these since my youth." Jesus, looking at him, loved him and said, "You lack one thing; go, sell whatever you own, and give the money to the poor and you will have treasure in heaven; then come, follow me." When he heard this, he was shocked and went away grieving, for he had many possessions.*

Eric Law in his book, *Holy Currencies*, writes about this encounter between Jesus and the rich man:

> *The rich man went away sad because he could not see and even imagine the fuller vision of the Cycle of Blessings. He could not see how resources would return to him once he gave them up. This invitation to give forces the rich to trust the abundance that God provides. It is in the rhythm of giving and receiving, living rich and living poor, that we learn to live according to God's vision of the world.*[1]

1. Law, *Holy Currencies*, 135.

For most of us in America the conclusion of that quote sounds strange, right? What does Law mean by "living rich and living poor"? That is not the American way of life, is it? More descriptive of our way of life is the theme song from the 1970's sitcom, *The Jeffersons*: "We're Movin' on Up." "And besides," we might say, "I'm not among the rich." Yet research shows that, as of 2011—despite the shrinking of America's middle class—88% of Americans still qualified as either upper-middle income or high income when viewed on a global scale.[2]

Invite the group to discuss and respond to the questions below:

- *Have you ever experienced the truth of Law's words? Have you ever given up something of value to you, something that felt risky, only to receive something greater down the road?*

- *Have you ever lived through a "season" of financial need? Did it impact your ability to appreciate "simple gifts" and to be generous with others?*

- *If you have lived through cycles of "living rich" and "living poor," what lessons did you learn as a result?*

John Wesley, founder of the Methodist Church, issued the challenge that if—at the time of his death—he was found to have more than 10 pounds in his keeping, all were welcome to call him a thief and a liar. True to his word, at his passing, Wesley was found to have nothing more than some loose spending money and six pounds set aside to compensate the poor men who would carry his body to the cemetery. If one factors in inflation and the exchange rate from pound to dollar, John Wesley gave away nearly half a million dollars in his lifetime.

Wesley laid out three simple rules regarding money in his sermon "On the Use of Money":[3]

1. *Gain all you can.* Wesley had a strong work ethic and encouraged the Methodists to be industrious, but never to a degree that impacted their own well-being or the well-being of others. Wesley admonished them to "gain all you can" without harming your health, your mind, or your neighbor.

   Consider our current culture. How might Americans live differently if they set these healthy boundaries around their work? Does your work ever negatively impact your physical or emotional health or your relationships? [Give the group time to reflect and respond]

2. *Save all you can.* Wesley's second rule is often misunderstood. By "saving," Wesley was not talking about a savings account or other forms of investing. By "saving" he meant to discourage irresponsible, frivolous spending. We might compare

---

2. Kochhar, "How Americans compare with the global middle class."
3. Sugden, "The Use of Money," 636–45.

this to the more contemporary admonishment: "Live simply so others can simply live."

Consider our culture and marketing. We are encouraged to buy whatever we can afford, even things we cannot afford. Do you ever struggle to live simply? Do you ever examine your life and realize that you have wasted your resources on something you didn't really need and something that, ultimately, did not bring you the joy you'd hoped for? [Give the group time to reflect and respond.]

3. *Give all you can.* By this Wesley was not limiting his instruction to tithing (a giving of 10%). By this, he encouraged the early Methodists to live a generous lifestyle out of trust in God and compassion for others.

How do you make decisions about how much to give? Is your giving based on a number or a percentage, or does your giving reflect what remains at the end of the month after all your expenses are paid? Do you give because you emotionally identify with a particular need or simply because it seems like the right thing to do? What criteria do you find most helpful in determining your own level of generosity? [Give the group time to reflect and respond.]

Our attitude toward giving also shines light on how we view ourselves. In a seminary course on "Faith and Finances," Dr. Leonard Sweet (preacher, speaker, and author) pointed out that, as Christians, we like to think of ourselves as givers. And yet, to name ourselves as Christians requires the recognition that *our identity begins with receiving.*[4] We are Christians precisely because we have embraced God's gift of grace.

Why is it important to embrace our identity as receivers? Does this understanding impact or influence our giving? If so, why and how? Do you think our own recognition of our need for God's grace impacts our ability to be generous and merciful with others? [Give participants time to share their thoughts.]

Before closing the group time, inquire if this week's reading caused participants to think differently about generosity. Ask if any questions were raised in their reading that we did not address in our discussion.

Let group members know that, in this coming week, they will be asked to write a spiritual autobiography. Their reading will help them understand what this means. Encourage them to complete their reading early in the week so they have ample time to write out their spiritual autobiography. Let them know that their autobiography *should be written out or drawn* (if they prefer to express themselves in pictures) and brought with them to the next group session.

Furthermore, they should expect next week's group time to last slightly longer: perhaps about 15 minutes longer than usual (depending on group size). They should plan their schedule accordingly.

4. Lecture notes taken by the author during a course offered at United Theological Seminary in Dayton, Ohio.

Close with words from the Apostle Paul to the church in Philippi. Using an early Christian hymn found in chapter 2 (verses 6–11), Paul concludes with these words about the generous, sacrificial giving of Christ who

> though he was in the form of God, did not regard equality with God as something to be exploited; but emptied himself, taking the form of a slave, being born in human likeness. And being found in human form, he humbled himself and became obedient to the point of death—even death on a cross. Therefore God also highly exalted him and gave him the name that is above every name, so that at the name of Jesus every knee will bend, in heaven and on earth and under the earth, and every tongue will confess that Jesus Christ is Lord, to the glory of God the Father.

Extinguish the candle.

Session 5

(ITEMS NEEDED: A CANDLE and Bible)

Review the group covenant by inviting a participant to read the covenant aloud (provided in Appendix C).

Remind the group of the format for each session:

- Light a candle

- Hear a word of scripture

- Take a few moments to breathe deeply and relax

- Have a time of prayer that will conclude with the Lord's Prayer.

Light the candle and explain that it is a reminder to us of Jesus' presence with us, since Jesus is the light of the world. Read this scripture from Psalm 139:1, 13, 15–16:

> *O Lord, you have searched me and known me . . . For it was you who formed my inward parts; you knit me together in my mother's womb . . . My frame was not hidden from you, when I was being made in secret, intricately woven in the depths of the earth. Your eyes beheld my unformed substance. In your book were written all the days that were formed for me, when none of them as yet existed.*

Invite participants to take a few moments to close their eyes and breathe deeply and slowly, using these moments to begin to relax and let go of the day's tensions.

Invite participants to name anyone or any situation for which they desire prayer. All they need to do is speak the name of the one in need, since God already knows every need. Let them know that the prayer time will conclude with the Lord's Prayer.

Remind participants that this week's format will be different than that of previous weeks. At this session, each member of the group will be asked to share a portion from their spiritual autobiography that they compiled during the week. *You will want to begin since your willingness to be open and vulnerable with the group will set the tone for everyone who follows.*

Let them know that, at the conclusion of each individual's sharing, other members of the group will reflect back what they have heard. However, this will not be a time of judgment or advice giving. When we share our stories, we make ourselves vulnerable to one another. Henri Nouwen writes, "After everything has been said and done, what we have to offer is our authentic selves in relationship to others."[1] Group members will be invited to affirm what they hear in one another's stories, and particularly to identify where or how they saw evidence of God's grace expressed in the "autobiographer's" journey.

Those who tell their story will also be invited to share with the group:

- What was the easiest part of this process?

- What was most difficult?

- What new insights into your life and your walk with God were revealed to you as you engaged in this process?

Let group members know that, as they respond to the story of the one who has shared, *we need to resist the temptation to talk about ourselves*—to point out similarities or make comparisons. Each person will have a turn to share their journey. To simply listen to someone is a wonderful gift. It is a way of honoring them. As we respond to what others have shared, "I" statements can be an indicator that we have moved the focus away from the person who shared and onto ourselves: e.g., "I've felt like that too when . . ."

Resist the impulse to ask questions out of curiosity. Questions are only appropriate if they help the one who shared to more deeply explore their journey and God's presence with them along the journey.

Furthermore, this is not a time to ask questions about other people or places referenced in the "autobiographer's" story. For example, if they note that the illness of a close friend first prompted them to consider their own aging and vulnerability, we don't want to stray off topic by asking questions like "How is your friend doing now?" or "I hear there are some wonderful new medications for treating that condition. Has he tried them?" etc.

Finally, do not offer advice. Advice giving in this context can violate trust and the sacred gift of vulnerability.

After listeners have responded and the one who shared has also responded, ask if anyone would like to pray for the individual who has just shared their story.

After everyone in the group has had the opportunity to share a portion of their autobiography, engage with the group, and be prayed over, invite members to take some time in silence to inwardly reflect on what they have heard and experienced in this sacred time of sharing.

---

1. Nouwen, *Spiritual Direction*, 10.

After a few moments of silence, read these words from Psalm 139, verses 23–24: *Search me, O God, and know my heart; test me and know my thoughts. See if there is any hurtful² way in me, and lead me in the way everlasting.*

Extinguish the candle.

End with this traditional Gaelic blessing:

May the road rise to meet you,

May the wind be always at your back,

May the sun shine warm upon your face,

May the rains fall soft upon your fields,

May God hold you in the palm of his hand. Amen.³

2. General translation is "wicked." The NRSV notes an alternative translation of "hurtful." "Hurtful" is used here because it is a relational, rather than an abstract, term.

3. This version of the blessing is found in *The United Methodist Book of Worship*, #565.

Session 6

(ITEMS NEEDED: CANDLE, BIBLE, anointing oil is optional)

Review the group covenant by inviting a participant to read the covenant aloud (see Appendix C).

Remind the group of the format for each session:

- Light a candle

- Hear a word of scripture

- Take a few moments to breathe deeply and relax

- Have a time of prayer that will conclude with the Lord's Prayer.

Light the candle and explain that it is a reminder to us of Jesus' presence with us, since Jesus is the light of the world. Read this scripture based on 1 Corinthians 12:4–7:

> Now there are varieties of gifts, but the same Spirit; and there are varieties of
> services, but the same Lord; and there are varieties of activities, but it is the same
> God who activates all of them in everyone. To each is given the manifestation of
> the Spirit for the common good.

Invite members to take a few moments to close their eyes and breathe deeply and slowly, using the time to begin to relax and let go of the day's tensions.

Invite group members to name anyone or any situation for which they desire prayer. All they need to do is speak the name of the one in need, since God already knows every need. Let them know that the prayer time will conclude with the Lord's Prayer.

Remind members that this week we were asked to spend some time reflecting on our past in order to better discern God's will for our future and the call God places upon our lives. Together we considered:

- Our *talents*

- Our *service* to those in need

- Those things that delight us or bring us *joy*

- Those things that evoke our *compassion*

Invite participants to each take a turn discussing their reflection on *one* of the four things listed above. Instruct the group that individuals will share as they are ready. Each person's time of sharing will be followed by a brief time of silence to better reflect on what has been shared. Then, other members of the group are invited to identify ways in which they have seen evidence of the particular skill, service, joy, or compassion that was shared. Finally, group members are invited to gather around the one who shared and offer a prayer on their behalf related to what has been shared. Let participants know that, in scripture, anointing can "signify the consecration, or setting apart, of someone for a holy purpose."[1] When we willingly offer up to God our skills, our service, and our whole selves, they are consecrated, or set apart, for God's purposes.

After giving that explanation, let members of your group know that they may be anointed, if they so desire.

Note: If anointing is not a part of someone's religious tradition, it may feel awkward and strange. Likewise, not all persons are comfortable being touched, even by those they know. Ask individuals what they are comfortable with and respond accordingly. The laying on of hands and anointing should only be done if individuals are comfortable with these practices.

After each participant has had the opportunity to share and reflect, let participants know that, as a conclusion to this six-week study, you will guide them through a meditation on scripture that will allow them to reflect on their experiences during this study. Invite participants to listen as you read the story of the loaves and the fishes recorded in Mark 6:30–44.

> *30 The apostles returned to Jesus and told him all that they had done and taught. 31 And he said to them, "Come away by yourselves to a desolate place and rest a while." For many were coming and going, and they had no leisure even to eat. 32 And they went away in the boat to a desolate place by themselves. 33 Now many saw them going and recognized them, and they ran there on foot from all the towns and got there ahead of them. 34 When he went ashore he saw a great crowd, and he had compassion on them, because they were like sheep without a shepherd. And he began to teach them many things. 35 And when it grew late, his disciples came to him and said, "This is a desolate place, and the hour is now late. 36 Send them away to go into the surrounding countryside and villages and buy themselves something to eat." 37 But he answered them, "You give them something to eat." And they said to him, "Shall we go and buy two hundred denarii worth of bread and give it to them to eat?" 38 And he said to them, "How*

---

1. Powell, *Harper Collins*, 33.

many loaves do you have? Go and see." And when they had found out, they said, "Five, and two fish." 39 Then he commanded them all to sit down in groups on the green grass. 40 So they sat down in groups, by hundreds and by fifties. 41 And taking the five loaves and the two fish he looked up to heaven and said a blessing and broke the loaves and gave them to the disciples to set before the people. And he divided the two fish among them all. 42 And they all ate and were satisfied. 43 And they took up twelve baskets full of broken pieces and of the fish. 44 And those who ate the loaves were five thousand men.

Let participants know that you will read the story a second time, this time pausing to pose questions after portions of the story. Encourage them to take their time to share their responses to the questions posed. Let them know that we'll not discuss our responses (i.e., no "cross-talking"). We will simply offer our responses and quietly receive the responses of others. If the participants in this group are all part of the same faith community, the bulleted questions that are bracketed may also be used.

Mark 6:30 The apostles returned to Jesus and told him all that they had done and taught. 31 And he said to them, "Come away by yourselves to a desolate place and rest a while." For many were coming and going, and they had no leisure even to eat. 32 And they went away in the boat to a desolate place by themselves.

The word "desolate" is a translation of the Greek word *eremos*. It means a place that is uninhabited, isolated, or empty. Particularly in Mark's gospel, Jesus seeks out these uninhabited places so that he may have quiet time alone in prayer.

- How have you experienced this spiritual study together as "desolate space:" a quiet, open space to get away for prayer, reflection, and sharing over these past six weeks?
- Do you ever feel like you "pass yourself coming and going?"
- How has this group allowed you to pause and center yourself?
  [Pause here for reflection and participant response]

Mark 6:33 Now many saw them going and recognized them, and they ran there on foot from all the towns and got there ahead of them. 34 When Jesus went ashore he saw a great crowd, and he had compassion on them, because they were like sheep without a shepherd. And he began to teach them many things.

The people sought Jesus out to minister to their needs.

- What are some of the needs people in our community have?
- What might they be seeking?
- How do we demonstrate compassion toward them?
- [How does our church demonstrate compassion?]

[Pause here for reflection and participant response]

> *Mark 6:35 And when it grew late, his disciples came to him and said, "This is a desolate place, and the hour is now late. 36 Send them away to go into the surrounding countryside and villages and buy themselves something to eat." 37 But he answered them, "You give them something to eat." And they said to him, "Shall we go and buy two hundred denarii worth of bread and give it to them to eat?" 38 And he said to them, "How many loaves do you have? Go and see." And when they had found out, they said, "Five, and two fish."*

Imagine the fear and the panic on the part of the disciples.

- Have you ever felt fear or anxiety that you do not have adequate resources to respond to the needs of others? [Pause here for reflection and participant response]

- [In what ways does our congregation demonstrate fear or anxiety that we will not have enough to meet people's needs?]
  [Pause here for reflection and participant response]

> *Mark 6:39 Then he commanded them all to sit down in groups on the green grass. 40 So they sat down in groups, by hundreds and by fifties. 41 And taking the five loaves and the two fish he looked up to heaven and said a blessing and broke the loaves and gave them to the disciples to set before the people. And he divided the two fish among them all. 42 And they all ate and were satisfied. 43 And they took up twelve baskets full of broken pieces and of the fish. 44 And those who ate the loaves were five thousand men.*

Through this story we discover that our meager resources in the hands of Jesus are more than enough to meet the needs of a hungry world.

- How has this week's focus on spiritual gifts and God's call changed or impacted your perspective on what you are able to do to carry out God's mission in the world? [pause here for reflection and participant response]

- [Have you, through the affirmation of this group, discovered a new gift or passion that you can use to support our church in carrying out its mission?]
  [Pause here for reflection and participant response]

Invite participants to turn to page 57. Close the group with everyone praying in unison this Covenant Prayer attributed to John Wesley:

> "I am no longer my own, but thine.
> Put me to what thou wilt, rank me with whom thou wilt.
> Put me to doing, put me to suffering.
> Let me be employed by thee or laid aside for thee,
> exalted for thee or brought low for thee.
> Let me be full, let me be empty.

Let me have all things, let me have nothing.

I freely and heartily yield all things

to thy pleasure and disposal.

And now, O glorious and blessed God,

Father, Son, and Holy Spirit,

thou art mine, and I am thine. So be it.

And the covenant which I have made on earth,

let it be ratified in heaven. Amen."

Extinguish the candle.

Conclude with this benediction from Numbers 6:24–26:

The Lord bless you and keep you; the Lord make his face to shine upon you and be gracious to you; the Lord lift up his countenance upon you and give you peace. Amen.

Appendix A

The Lord's Prayer in Four Different Versions/Translations

The New Revised Standard Version (NRSV)

[Jesus said:] "Pray then in this way: Our Father in heaven, hallowed be your name.

Your kingdom come. Your will be done, on earth as it is in heaven.

Give us this day our daily bread.

And forgive us our debts, as we also have forgiven our debtors.

And do not bring us to the time of trial, but rescue us from the evil one."

The New International Version (NIV)

[Jesus said:] "This, then, is how you should pray: 'Our Father in heaven, hallowed be your name,

your kingdom come, your will be done on earth as it is in heaven.

Give us today our daily bread.

Forgive us our debts, as we also have forgiven our debtors.

And lead us not into temptation, but deliver us from the evil one.'"

The King James Version

[Jesus said:] "After this manner therefore pray ye:

Our Father which art in heaven, Hallowed be thy name.

Thy kingdom come. Thy will be done in earth, as *it is* in heaven.

Give us this day our daily bread.

And forgive us our debts, as we forgive our debtors.

And lead us not into temptation, but deliver us from evil."

The Message (MSG)

[Jesus said]: "You can pray very simply. Like this:

Our Father in heaven, reveal who you are.

Set the world right; do what's best—as above, so below.

Keep us alive with three square meals.

Keep us forgiven with you and forgiving others.

Keep us safe from ourselves and the Devil."

Appendix B

Three Types of Prayer

Developing a Breath Prayer:[1]

Step 1: Close your eyes and focus on your breathing.

Step 2: Imagine God is calling you by name. God is asking of you as Jesus asked of his disciples long ago, "What are you looking for? What are you seeking?"

Step 3: Respond to God. What is it that you are seeking; what are you yearning for most in your life?

Step 4: Think of the various names or titles for God—Father, Mighty God, Good Shepherd, Savior, etc. Choose the name or title that means the most to you.

Step 5: Combine the name and what you are seeking into one phrase—e.g., "Good Shepherd, lead and guide me."

The Prayer of Examen:[2]

Gift: What gifts have I received or given over the past few days; in other words, when did I give the gift of love to another, and when did I receive the gift of love from someone else?

---

1. The form presented here has been adapted from Barton, *Sacred Rhythms*, 76, with the permission of InterVarsity Press.

2. The form presented here has been adapted from Brown, *Paths to Prayer*, 187, with Brown's written consent.

Struggle: Over the past few days, recall a time or times when you failed to give and receive love; recall times when you may have felt anxious or restless about unresolved issues.

Invitation: Now, ask yourself, "what gift or kindness would I seek from God in order to move forward in an attitude of peace and wholeness?" What, among God's many mercies (for example, God's forgiveness, God's strength, God's comfort), do you most need from God today? *Conclude* by breathing slowly and resting in God's grace.

A Prayer of Blessing:[3]

May your ears be blessed that you may hear the gospel of Christ, which is the Word of life.

May your eyes be blessed that you may see the light of Christ as he illumines your way.

May your lips be blessed that you may sing the praise of Christ, the joy of the Church.

May your heart be blessed that God may dwell there by faith.

May your shoulders be blessed that they may bear the gentle yoke of Jesus.

May your hands be blessed so that God's mercy may be known through your actions.

May your feet be blessed that you may walk in the way of Christ. Amen.

---

3. The blessing presented here has been adapted from a Protestant baptismal prayer.

Appendix C

Group Covenant

OUR GROUP WILL ABIDE by a covenant. A covenant is an agreement that defines *how* we'll be in relationship with one another. For this group to be a safe and meaningful experience, we'll need to all agree to:

- Be on time and be regular in attendance.

- Be authentic in our presentation of ourselves.

- Be respectful in communication by:

    ◆ Speaking only on behalf of ourselves

    ◆ Listening more than we speak

    ◆ Receiving what others say and share, even if we disagree

- Appreciate, and not be anxious, with silence.

- Maintain confidentiality.

- Allow others to speak and share as they are willing and when they are ready.

- Avoid the desire to "fix or correct someone." Only God can change our hearts and minds. And only God really knows us and knows the areas of our life where growth and change are needed.

- Seek clarification and don't make assumptions.

- Only give advice when it is expressly requested (in other words, in response to another's expressed request to receive rather than our desire to give).

- Pray for one another.

Bibliography

Barton, Ruth Haley. *Sacred Rhythms: Arranging Our Lives for Spiritual Transformation.* Downers Grove, IL: InterVarsity, 2006.

Brown, Patricia D. *Paths to Prayer: Finding Your Own Way to the Presence of God.* San Francisco, CA: Wiley, 2003.

Bryant, Stephen D., et al., eds. *Companions in Christ: A Small-Group Experience in Spiritual Formation.* Nashville: Upper Room, 2006.

deSilva, David A. "Grace." In *Eerdmans Dictionary of the Bible*, edited by David Noel Freedman, Allen C. Myers, and Astrid B. Beck, 524–26. Grand Rapids, MI: W.B. Eerdmans, 2000.

———. *An Introduction to the New Testament: Contexts, Methods and Ministry Formation.* 2nd ed. Downers Grove, IL: InterVarsity, 2018.

Foster, Richard J. *Celebration of Discipline: The Path to Spiritual Growth.* New York: HarperCollins, 1978.

Freedman, David Noel, et al. *Eerdmans Dictionary of the Bible.* Grand Rapids, MI: W.B. Eerdmans, 2000.

Gaventa, Beverly Roberts, and David Petersen, eds. *The New Interpreter's Bible: One Volume Commentary.* Nashville: Abingdon, 2010.

Hess, Lisa M. *Artisanal Theology: Intentional Formation in Radically Covenantal Companionship.* Eugene, OR: Wipf and Stock, 2009.

Kochhar, Rakesh. "How Americans Compare with the Global Middle Class." Pew Research Center, July 9, 2015. https://www.pewresearch.org/fact-tank/2015/07/09/how-americans-compare-with-the-global-middle-class/.

Law, Eric H. F. *Holy Currencies: 6 Blessings for Sustainable Missional Ministries.* St. Louis: Chalice, 2013.

McCann, J. Clinton, Jr. "The Book of Psalms." In *The New Interpreter's Bible: A Commentary in Twelve Volumes*, 4: 639–1280. Nashville: Abingdon, 1996.

Nouwen, Henri. *Spiritual Direction: Wisdom for the Long Walk of Faith.* New York: HarperCollins, 2006.

Nowell, Irene. *Pleading, Cursing, Praising: Conversing with God through the Psalms.* Collegeville, MN: Liturgical, 2013.

Outler, Albert, ed. *John Wesley.* Oxford: Oxford University Press, 1964.

Peace, Richard. *Spiritual Journaling: Recording Your Journey Toward God.* Colorado Springs, CO: NavPress, 1998.

Sugden, Edward H., ed. "The Use of Money." In *John Wesley's Fifty-Three Sermons*, 632–46. Nashville: Abingdon, 1988.

The United Methodist Hymnal: Book of United Methodist Worship. Nashville: The United Methodist Publishing House, 1989.

Theissen, Gerd. *The Social Setting of Pauline Christianity: Essays on Corinth*. Philadelphia: Fortress, 1982.

Willimon, William. "The God We Hardly Knew." In *Watch for the Light: Readings for Advent and Christmas*, 141–49. Farmington, PA: Plough, 2001.

www.ingramcontent.com/pod-product-compliance
Lightning Source LLC
LaVergne TN
LVHW081325060426
835511LV00011B/1871